Steve Parish
NATURE Kids
KOALAS

MY FIRST
PICTURE
BOOK

www.steveparish.com.au

Koalas live only in Australia. They are most often found in gum trees. Koalas grow fur all over their bodies. Like humans, they breathe air and have warm blood.

Koalas belong to a group of animals called marsupials. A female marsupial has a pouch on her belly. Her tiny baby grows up in this pouch.

Koalas have strong claws. They have two thumbs on each of their front paws. This helps them to grip onto the trunks of trees easily.

Koalas give birth to babies that have no fur and cannot see. When a baby is born, it crawls through its mother's fur to her pouch.

Inside the pouch, the baby finds a nipple. It stays attached to the nipple until it has grown fur and can see.

After about seven months, the baby starts to climb out of the pouch and wander close to its mother.

A koala's fur is soft, fine and thick to keep it warm.
Its fur is waterproof so the koala stays dry when it rains.

Koalas spend most of their time asleep in the forks of gum trees. They don't need to be alert for danger. There are few enemies climbing in the trees.

When a koala is not asleep, it is usually eating gum leaves. Koalas have to eat a lot of leaves because the leaves do not give the koalas much energy.

Sometimes a koala needs to move to a different tree to find more food. It climbs down to the ground and runs on all four limbs to another tree.

Because their gum leaf diet does not give them much energy, koalas sleep a lot. They need to save their energy for climbing and keeping warm.

When the weather is cold, a koala will curl itself up into a ball to keep itself warm. In hot weather, a koala will stretch out its limbs so that it can feel any cool breezes.

Koalas live in eastern Australia. They were once found in other areas, but they were hunted by humans. Koalas have since been brought back to some of these areas to live.

Areas where koalas live need to be protected because, without gum trees, koalas have no food and no homes.

A koala

clings to its mother's back

is protected by thick fur

can see during day or night

smells the leaves it has picked carefully before eating them

uses two thumbs and three fingers to grip branches

has only a stub of a tail

Some zoos & fauna parks

QUEENSLAND
Cairns
Undersea World
Townsville
Great Barrier Reef Aquarium
Mooloolaba
Underwater World
Brisbane
Lone Pine Koala Sanctuary
Currumbin
Currumbin Sanctuary
Burleigh
Fleays Wildlife Park

NORTHERN TERRITORY
Berry Springs
Territory Wildlife Park
Alice Springs
Desert Wildlife Park

WESTERN AUSTRALIA
Perth
Perth Zoo
Hillarys
Underwater World
Karnup
Marapana Wildlife World

SOUTH AUSTRALIA
Adelaide
Adelaide Zoo
Mt Lofty
Cleland Wildlife Park
Mylor
Warrawong Sanctuary
Monarto
Monarto Zoo

VICTORIA
Melbourne
Melbourne Zoo
Healesville Sanctuary
Werribee Zoo
Phillip Island
Phillip Island Wildlife Park
Penguin Reserve
Seal Rocks

NEW SOUTH WALES
Dubbo
Western Plains Zoo
Sydney
Taronga Zoo
Sydney Aquarium

ACT
Canberra
Tidbinbilla Nature Reserve

TASMANIA
Brighton
Bonorong Park Wildlife Centre
Cygnet
Talune Wildlife Park & Koala Gardens
Mole Creek
Trowunna Wildlife Park